THE

GHOSTLY TALES

OF

NANTUCKET

Published by Arcadia Children's Books
A Division of Arcadia Publishing
Charleston, SC
www.arcadiapublishing.com

Spooky America is a trademark of Arcadia Publishing, Inc.

First published 2024
Manufactured in the United States

Designed by Jessica Nevins
Images used courtesy of Shutterstock.com.

ISBN: 978-1-4671-9762-5

Library of Congress Control Number: 2024930951

Notice: The information in this book is true and complete to the best of our knowledge. It is offered without guarantee on the part of the author or Arcadia Publishing. The author and Arcadia Publishing disclaim all liability in connection with the use of this book.

THE
GHOSTLY TALES
OF
NANTUCKET

PATRICIA HEYER

Adapted from *Haunted Nantucket* by Barbara Sillery

MASSACHUSETTS

NANTUCKET

ATLANTIC OCEAN

NANTUCKET HARBOR

TABLE OF CONTENTS & MAP KEY

Welcome to
Spooky Nantucket!

Do you like spooky stories? Do you smile when you read about ghosts? Are you curious about the spirits that haunt the island of Nantucket? If so, *The Ghostly Tales of Nantucket* is for you.

It doesn't matter if you live on the island full time or if this is your first visit. If you keep your eyes open as you explore, you will surely meet up with creepy and mysterious spirits, perhaps even hair-raising phantoms.

Some of these hauntings have been around since Nantucket's earliest days, when the island was home to Indigenous peoples. Others are from the nineteenth century, when Nantucket was the world's whaling capital. There are ghosts from the great fire of 1846, as well as the spirits of many famous locals who have chosen to remain even after their deaths.

You can meet these ghostly phantoms and learn more about their antics in this book. You will witness their most recent sightings and even meet the ghosts of famous old-time islanders who have decided to stay forever. There are hauntings in hotels and inns all across the island that keep people awake at night. Some spirits float along the hotel corridors, while others play old-time music, move things around, and open and close windows.

You may meet a 200-year-old pastor just by visiting an old church. But be on your best behavior—he can be grouchy. You might spy on a trio of ghosts as they smuggle rum into the back of a local restaurant. Perhaps you'll even encounter some of Nantucket's most outspoken ghosts by watching the hologram presentation at the Whaling Museum.

A famous ghostly story from the island tells of a foolish sea captain who chased a crooked-jaw whale only to be led astray by a mermaid. Another often-seen ghost on Nantucket is that of George Pollard, known as the island's unluckiest captain. Although Captain Pollard survived being shipwrecked and stranded when a whale rammed and sank his ship, his next command also ended in tragedy. Just a few years later, Captain Pollard was shipwrecked again after his ship hit the rocks off a small island in the Pacific Ocean. He never went back to sea, and some say his restless spirit still lingers. On foggy nights, his withered and frail apparition appears with an old whale-oil lantern in one hand as he wanders the streets and waterfront of Nantucket.

These spooky tales may keep you up at night, but they'll also explain why Nantucket is one of the most haunted islands in the North Atlantic.

You will find a little bonus at the end of each spooky story called Nantucket Tidbits.

Each "tidbit" will tell you a bit more about the people, places, or hauntings from the chapter.

Happy reading! The ghosts can't wait to meet you!

CHAPTER 1

The Rocking Chair Ghost

Did you know Nantucket was the world's whaling capital for over 200 years? In those days, people didn't come to the island for a restful summer vacation. They came to work. Many wanted to "go to sea" as crewmembers on one of Nantucket's famous whaling ships. Some came alone, renting rooms in one of the many boarding houses along the shore. Others came with their families. Soon, houses, schools, stores, and churches popped up across the island.

You would be surprised to see what Nantucket's harbor looked like in 1800. The town had no coffee houses, stylish restaurants, or plush hotels. The harbor was dirty, sooty, and quite smelly. Factories, workshops, and whale blubber processing plants lined the waterfront.

It was a busy harbor full of ships, seamen, and workers. Everywhere you looked, you could see dozens of carpenters building or repairing ships and boats of all sizes. Local carpenters also created replacement parts for ships, furniture, tools, and coffins. Coopers— men who made waterproof barrels, buckets, and casks for whale oil—were in high demand. Blacksmiths, too, worked along the harbor, making harpoons, knives, anchor chains, or anything a ship may need.

Since each whale ship required enormous amounts of rope, miles of rope in all sizes were created in factories along the harbor. Sailmakers were also in high demand. Giant sail-making workshops called lofts dotted the island. Sails will not work correctly on a sailing vessel unless they fit perfectly. So, every ship needed twenty to thirty sails for their voyage.

Whaling ships carried everything they could possibly need for a two-year voyage. That included food, water, medicine, clothes, candles, lamp oil, and even spare parts for the ship. They even brought extra wood to build coffins in case someone died. On the ships, they also transported the small six-man whaleboats and weapons needed for the whale hunt. There was equipment onboard to boil the whale blubber into oil, and the waterproof barrels needed to store their precious cargo. Workshops and factories along the waterfront used whale products to make things like candles, usable oils, waxes, and perfumes.

Over the years, Nantucket changed. Whaling became more difficult. Captains had to take their ships on longer voyages because so many of the whales in nearby waters had been killed. Nantucket's popularity as a whaling center shrank when the railroad came to the mainland.

Today, Nantucket is a popular summer destination. The once-overcrowded, dirty harbor is now a beautiful marina filled with dozens of colorful watercraft and visitors from across the globe.

Although many newcomers are surprised to hear that Nantucket is haunted, most islanders have known it for years.

They often share their encounters with the many ghosts that share their home and island. Don't be surprised if you meet some of these spirited Nantucketers during your stay.

You might find a ghost in the Jared Coffin House, a popular hotel in downtown Nantucket. The beautiful three-story red-brick building has stood on Broad Street for over 175 years. At the height of the whaling days, Jared Coffin, a wealthy shipbuilder, built the mansion for his family. Although he loved the beautiful home, his wife disliked living on the island so much that they moved back to the mainland after less than a year.

After the Coffins sold their home, it became a hotel known as Ocean House. It welcomed many famous people, including Herman Melville, author of the classic novel, *Moby Dick*, and President Ulysses S. Grant. Today, it is one of the most popular hotels on Nantucket, known as the Jared Coffin House.

Like many buildings in the area, the beautiful mansion is both a historic site and a business. Not everyone knows that it also hosts more than its share of ghosts.

The mansion has welcomed thousands of guests since it opened. So, it is no surprise that many different phantoms roam the halls of the old building and make themselves at home in the beautiful guestrooms. Some visitors say that grayish clouds suddenly appear in their rooms, only to quickly vanish. Others report seeing solid figures that look very much alive, but who seem unaware of the living.

A pale, sad-looking little

girl appears suddenly to astonished guests in one room. She never speaks but stares at them as if they are intruders. She remains for a few minutes and then disappears.

In this same room, another guest once woke in the middle of the night to the spirit of a small child-like ghost poking her with an ice-cold finger. Though not everyone who stays there sees the little spirit, many report feeling as if someone is watching them.

One guest room on the second floor is always cold. Icy air sweeps across the room even on the hottest summer days. Visitors report that the frigid blast appears suddenly, sometimes waking them from a deep sleep.

One of the best-known ghosts at the Jared Coffin House is the spirit of a former housekeeper named Phoebe. Although she passed away many years ago, the stern, no-nonsense housekeeper remains at the hotel. She keeps an eye on the staff to be sure they do their work correctly, and if she sees guests misbehaving, she does not hesitate to scold them!

The most famous ghost spotted here is the specter of the former owner, Jared Coffin. Although he has been dead for hundreds of years, he returns to the beautiful mansion he built so long ago. Many guests report a well-dressed old man sitting in the rocking chair on chilly afternoons. The apparition stares out the window without speaking to anyone. He never answers if spoken to and vanishes if someone comes too close to the chair. Local legends say that Jared Coffin was unhappy when his wife insisted they leave Nantucket. They believe that now that he is dead, he has returned to Nantucket to the house he loved.

Should you visit the Jared Coffin House, look for the rocking chair. Take a peek to see if he is sitting there. But don't be disappointed if he doesn't greet you.

NANTUCKET TIDBITS:

- The "Great Fire" of 1846 destroyed most of the town of Nantucket. Fueled by lumber and whale oil stored in the harbor, it swept across the town, destroying everything in its path. Hundreds lost their homes and jobs. Surprisingly, the Jared Coffin House not only survived the fire, but the brick and stone building also prevented the fire from spreading farther.

- You may think the name "Coffin" is unusual. But that is not the case on Nantucket. The Coffin family were among the very first settlers in the 1600s. You might say the sea was in their blood. Nearly everyone in the family made their living from the ocean. Some owned whale-related businesses

on the harbor; others were ship captains, crewmen, and explorers. Two family members discovered new islands while searching the faraway Pacific Ocean. Sadly, Owen Coffin was less fortunate. When a sperm whale rammed and sank his ship the *Essex* in 1902, he survived. However, he would later die at the hands of cannibals.

Noisy Spirits at the Nantucket Whaling Museum

Although there are half a dozen museums on the island, the best-known and busiest is the Nantucket Whaling Museum, located in the heart of town.

There is so much to see and do at the museum. You can get up close and personal with a thirty-six-foot sperm whale skeleton. You can eyeball the actual harpoons used on Nantucket's famous whaling ships or study the 200-year-old scrimshaw carvings created by local sailors during their long whaling voyages.

Nearby, you will find *The Tragedy of the Essex*, an exhibit dedicated to the loss of the historic Nantucket whaling ship. In 1820, captained by George Pollard, the *Essex* sank after being rammed by a giant sperm whale. Thirty years later, Herman Melville used the tragedy as the basis for his famous novel, *Moby Dick*. (You'll hear more about Captain Pollard in Chapter 5: Ghosts That Can't Say Goodbye.)

Another spooking-sounding exhibit here is *Spirits Among Us*, which uses laser-driven holograms to introduce visitors to a few of the spine-chilling hauntings reported on Nantucket. These are not ordinary ghosts, so be prepared to be surprised. These phantoms, apparitions, and ghostly spirits are deceased Nantucket women who left a mark on the island. The peculiar thing is that the museum is not the only place where you can meet these shadowy phantoms. They are spotted across Nantucket by anyone who knows their stories.

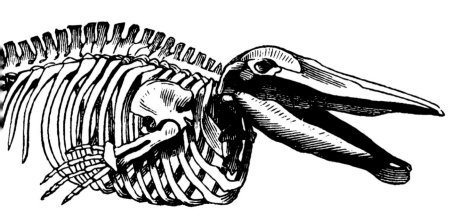

One of the ghosts is Mary Coffin Starbuck. She was among the earliest English settlers on the island. Although Mary had ten children, she was also an important church and community leader.

She was a deeply religious woman who insisted that rules be strictly followed. Known as "Great Mary," she was called to settle disagreements between neighbors and did not hesitate to scold anyone behaving badly.

It isn't surprising, then, that Mary's ghost is still here. Her bent-over figure, dressed in a worn gray robe, sometimes appears during church services on the island. She holds her hands over her ears whenever she hears loud music and wags her finger at girls dressed in skimpy bathing suits.

Other ghosts on the island include the spirits of Elizabeth Starbuck Barney and Anna Gardner. The two worked tirelessly to not only abolish slavery, but also for women's right to vote.

Elizabeth was known as a feisty woman who stood up for her beliefs. She was well-educated and loved science and history. Today, she haunts museums, libraries, and places of learning. She is a quiet ghost. She hovers in a corner just watching people as they read. If someone comes too near, she disappears.

Anna was from a well-to-do local family related to Benjamin Franklin. Although she loved living on Nantucket, she traveled widely, fighting for women's right to vote and promoting the abolition of slavery. Seriously injured in a carriage accident in New York City, she spent her last years sitting on her porch on Nantucket.

Should you encounter Anna, do not be surprised if she doesn't move around very much. Her ghost never leaves the porch.

You might spy on her peering into a newspaper, or in intense conversation with some invisible friend. If anyone comes too close, she vanishes.

Susan Veeder was probably the most widely traveled Nantucket woman of the nineteenth century. While Elizabeth and Anna were fighting to earn the right to vote, Susan was on a five-year voyage on a whaling ship with her husband. During that time, she sailed around Cape Horn, crossed the Pacific, and even sailed as far north as the Arctic.

Susan kept a journal during her travels, writing about life aboard the ship. She left nothing out, writing about the crew, accidents, arguments, illnesses, and even a mutiny. She drew colorful pictures of the unfamiliar people and places they visited. Today, her notebooks hold a special place in the historical collection at the museum.

Susan's ghost is often seen strolling along the waterfront in travel clothes, carrying her notebook and pencils. She stares out to sea, paying no attention to those around her. If someone calls out to her or comes too close, she evaporates.

Another phantom you may encounter on Nantucket is Kezia Folger Coffin. But be prepared! She is quite different from the other spirits you may meet here.

Keiza Folger Coffin lived on Nantucket during the American Revolution. Some called her a pirate, some called her a smuggler, and still others called her a traitor. She may have been all these things.

She was a cold-hearted woman who used her money and power to control life on the island. During the American Revolution, Kezia made a huge amount of money smuggling goods to the British.

When the Americans had begun to win the war, Keiza tried to switch sides, but she was convicted of treason, and her business went bankrupt. All her property, buildings, and goods were sold at an auction. Although charges were dropped after the war, Kezia never was able to recover her property.

Kezia's apparition began her hauntings soon after she died. Perhaps her ghost is trying to get back her money. Often, she appears to be directing her smuggling operation. Other times, she's seen at her old properties, trying to drive out the new owners. She moves things around, slams doors, and wakes people in the middle of the night. Kezia is an angry ghost. Although it is unlikely she will ever regain her property, it seems that she will never give up.

Another ghost you are likely to encounter

is that of Maria Mitchell. She was a teacher and librarian on Nantucket, as well as a skilled astronomer. She spent countless hours on the roof of the local bank peering into her small three-inch telescope. Her many hours of work were rewarded in 1847 when she discovered a new comet in the northern sky, later known as Miss Mitchell's Comet. She was the first female professional astronomer in the United States.

Over the years, Maria became quite famous. She traveled widely, studying and giving lectures at scientific seminars. She wrote for scientific journals and served as a professor at Vassar College. But above all, Maria loved living on Nantucket.

There is no doubt her ghost chose to remain on the island she loved. Maria looks like anyone else you might meet on Nantucket, except for her clothing. She wears an old-fashioned, high-necked dress that reaches her ankles.

Her hair is pulled back and neatly pinned under a small hat. She doesn't seem to notice that people are staring at her. But if you try to say hello, she'll vanish right before your eyes.

So don't be shocked if you happen to meet some of Nantucket's hometown phantoms. Ghostly spirits are among us on the island, and they are everywhere!

NANTUCKET TIDBITS:

- Holograms are created with computers using light and sound waves. These amazing devices bring the *Spirits Among Us* exhibit to life and share the story of a few of Nantucket's unforgettable courageous women.

- *Moby Dick*, a novel by Herman Melville, is one of the most famous books ever written.

It is a spellbinding adventure book you won't be able to put down. If you have not read it, don't walk, run to the library or bookstore! You will be glad you did.

Lay the Blame on Seth

What comes to your mind when you hear someone talk about Seth Swift? Unless you live on Nantucket, that name probably doesn't mean much to you. Seth doesn't live here anymore. In fact, he doesn't live anywhere. Seth died centuries ago. But that doesn't mean you won't come face-to-face with him on Nantucket!

Seth Swift is no ordinary ghost. More than 200 years ago, he was a living, breathing Nantucketer. Seth is one of the most famous ghosts on Nantucket. His main haunting spot is the historic Nantucket Universalist or South Church on Orange Avenue.

Seth was a well-respected pastor and community leader on the island for over twenty years. He became a legend across Nantucket for his compassion for people in need and the length of his Sunday sermons.

Yes, Seth liked to preach. His detailed, droning sermons were always more than an hour long. He read aloud long passages from the Bible and ended the Sunday service with

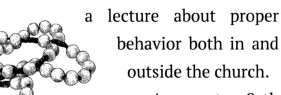

a lecture about proper behavior both in and outside the church.

As a pastor, Seth was well-known in

town and took his job very seriously. He took part in nearly every town event and insisted that everyone in the village follow the code of conduct outlined in his sermons. Seth could hear foul language blocks away and scolded anyone he heard telling a lie. It never came as a surprise to islanders when he corrected anyone using bad manners in public. Anyone who failed to conduct themselves like a lady or gentleman on the streets of Nantucket might not be allowed to take part in the church service or be banned from the church altogether.

Sightings of Seth's ghost began soon after he died and continue to this day. People report seeing him in nearly every part of the church. During winter, services are held in a smaller sanctuary in a basement area where a large portrait of Seth hangs along the side wall. According to many, his pale gray eyes stare straight ahead most of the time. But sometimes, they suddenly dart back and forth, glaring at people in the pews.

The sextants (helpers who work in the church doing repairs and keeping everything neat) often report peculiar experiences. One sextant was cleaning the pews when she heard footsteps coming closer. She knew it was Seth, so she began singing an old-time hymn as loudly as she could. The footsteps instantly stopped. Today, she never forgets to sing while working in the church, and Seth doesn't disturb her.

Seth is known to pound on the church's lower-level windows, demanding to be let inside. One sextant got so tired of all the hammering that he shouted, "Stop it, Seth, you're going to break the window." The pounding stopped immediately.

One frigid winter night, a worker was cleaning the kitchen when he heard three local kids tapping on the window. They said they were cold and asked to come inside to get warm. They began to shriek and chase one another as soon as they were inside. Before he could stop them, they charged up the stairs to the church's main floor. He could hear them running back and forth between the pews, screeching and shouting at one another. But then it suddenly became quiet. The trio came scrambling down the stairs the next moment, claiming that an old man had popped up from behind the pulpit and chased them away. There's no doubt it was Seth, for the old pastor never tolerated rowdy behavior from children.

It is well known that Seth does *not* like change. He was furious when the church added cameras and cell service. He was so annoyed that he blocked the tower door so the workers could not complete their tasks. He didn't give up easily, even clogging the passage to the choir loft.

Although most church members accept that the church is haunted, a few insist that the stories are just silly superstitions. They claim that people use the reports of the ghostly pastor to entice people to visit the church.

Most islanders take it for granted that the ghost of Seth Swift haunts South Church. The ghostly specter wants people to know he is there. He makes it known when he is unhappy with modern activities within the church, or when changes are made in the old historic building. Whenever items mysteriously move around by themselves or mysterious things happen for no reason, church staff just say, "Seth did it!"

NANTUCKET TIDBITS:

- The beautiful old church at 11 Orange Street opened its doors in 1809. Although it is officially called Nantucket Unitarian Universalist, most people just call it South Church.

- Although the church is over 200 years old, it has been updated many times. Its 109 foot tower is capped by a golden dome that can be spotted from nearly anywhere in town. The beautiful tower with its famous clock is often used as a landmark for visitors.

Not Everything Spooky Is a Ghost

This spooky tale from Nantucket is not about a haunted house, a nameless phantom lingering in the graveyard, or even an unsolved crime. In fact, there is not a single ghost in this story. It doesn't have creepy apparitions, nor are there unearthly noises at night. Rather, it is a legend that islanders have passed on for hundreds of years. This spooky story describes the life of Ichabod Paddock, a Nantucket whaler, and the events that drove him to flee the island for the safety of the mainland.

Ichabod Paddock came to Nantucket in 1609 to find work on a whaling ship. It wasn't long before everyone knew about Ichabod's astonishing skills. He was an expert when it came to catching whales. Soon, every whaling ship in Nantucket wanted him on their crew. He was so skillful that he trained newcomers how to chase and catch whales.

Ichabod was the talk of the town. People said he helped make Nantucket a famous whaling port. Before long, he became the captain of one of Nantucket's famous whaling ships.

As captain, Ichabod hunted whales in every ocean in the world. He crossed the Pacific's width and the equator more often than any other captain. He caught nearly every whale he hunted, except for one.

Despite everything he tried, Ichabod could not capture the crooked-jaw sperm whale that roamed the world's oceans. No one knew if the creature was injured or if it had been born that way. Other ship captains refused to hunt the whale with the deformed jaw because they considered it bad luck.

Ichabod was not superstitious. He was determined to catch the peculiar-looking beast. He tracked it for thousands of miles across the oceans for several years. Although he caught up with it many times, he could never capture it. Each time Ichabod's razor-sharp harpoons struck the whale, they merely bounced off its tough skin and fell into the sea. No matter how hard he tried, he could not catch the crooked-jawed whale.

By this time, Ichabod could talk of nothing but the whale. Whenever the ship's lookout shouted, "Thar she blows" (an expression sailors used to indicate that a whale was close by), Ichabod raced to the rail to see if it was the whale he wanted. No other whale would do.

Ichabod finally caught up with the whale not far from his home port of Nantucket. This time, he was determined not to fail. To hunt from a big whaling ship, sailors needed to get into a smaller boat called a whaleboat, which was stored on the ship. As the whaleboats were lowered for this final chase, Ichabod pushed his way to the bow of the lead boat. He would not miss this chance to kill the crooked-jaw whale with his own hands.

Once the six-man whaleboats grew near the whale, Ichabod grabbed hold of the largest and sharpest harpoon. He aimed for the whale's back. Once again, his blade bounced off the whale and dropped into the sea.

Ichabod couldn't believe his eyes. He shook his fists in the

air and reached for a knife. As his crew watched in horror, he raced to the side, leaped over the rail, and dived head-first into the ocean.

The moment he hit the water, the whale opened its crooked jaw, and Ichabod swam directly into the whale's enormous mouth. At first, everything was dark. Suddenly, Ichabod saw a large copper-colored door directly in his path. He reached for the handle and jerked it open.

Light streamed from the inside, revealing a beautifully decorated cabin. As Ichabod looked more closely, he saw two creatures sitting at a table playing cards. At the same moment, they both looked up at Ichabod. It was none other than the Devil himself and a beautiful golden-haired mermaid. The Devil glared at Ichabod for a moment, then vanished in a great black puff of smoke.

The beautiful mermaid smiled so sweetly at

Ichabod that he could not speak. He had never seen such an enchanting face in his life. Her skin was flittering green scales, and her lower body was a sparkling fishtail.

Meanwhile, Ichabod's crew waited for him to return. After nearly an hour of waiting, the crew argued about what they should do. Just when they agreed to return to port, the whale surged from the depths, just feet from their ship.

It opened its crooked jaw and spewed out Ichabod in a stream of gooey green slime. Not only was he unhurt, but he seemed to have enjoyed his journey into the great beast's body! Ichabod ordered the ship to port and declared they would return the next day.

Ichabod was true to his word. The following day, he ordered his ship back to the same spot. Waiting for him was the crooked-jawed whale.

Once again, Ichabod jumped into the chilly water and was immediately swallowed by the whale.

These strange events went on day after day. Ichabod stopped hunting whales. Instead, each day, he steered his ship to the same spot. Then, just as before, he plunged into the gaping mouth of the crooked-jaw whale. He was gone awhile, and then the great beast would reappear and spew him up in a smelly stream of greenish slime.

Ichabod never spoke about his time inside the belly of the whale, nor would he answer questions. Upon his return, he would order the ship back to port, then, with a broad smile, retreat to his private cabin.

The crew began to gossip among themselves about the captain's strange behavior. Ichabod was acting like a man possessed. Mariners knew that only a sailor bewitched by a mermaid could cause a man to act so foolishly. And that was exactly what had happened.

Rumors spread around the waterfront about Ichabod. It wasn't long before his wife learned what was going on. She was not about to lose her husband to the alluring mermaid. She knew just what to do.

One morning, when Ichabod arrived at the dock, he was carrying a beautiful silver harpoon with his initials stamped on the side. When the crew admired the beautiful shiny weapon, he explained that it had been a surprise gift from his wife.

As before, Ichabod's ship made straight for his meeting spot with the crooked-jawed whale. When they sighted the whale, his crew clamored for him to use his costly silver weapon to kill the great beast. Ichabod lifted the harpoon and halfheartedly tossed it in the direction of the whale. But this time, the moment it touched the whale, blood spurted into the air as the silver lance sliced through the skin of the giant beast. The creature let out one great whimper before rolling onto its side. The crooked-jawed whale was dead.

But the story doesn't end here. As often happens when a story is hundreds of years old, there is more than one ending.

According to one storyteller, the crew began to cut up the whale as soon as it died. They didn't find a bright copper-colored door or a cabin inside the whale's stomach. But most distressing to Ichabod, there was no sign of a mermaid.

Another account claims that the whale did not die. Instead, it plunged into the depths with Ichabod's silver harpoon dangling on its side. A few months later, another whaling ship captured and killed the crooked-jawed whale.

When they cut open its stomach, they found a silver harpoon with Ichabod's initials stamped along the side.

History tells us that Ichabod left Nantucket soon afterward. Some say he began to act so strangely after the whale died that he was chased off the island. Others say that the beautiful mermaid broke his heart, and so he returned to the mainland to die alone.

Nantucket Tidbits:

- Whaling ships were about one hundred feet long and twenty-five feet wide. They carried fifteen to forty men and all their provisions for a long sea journey. They also carried whaleboats and the tools and equipment to boil the whale blubber into oil. (The oil was stored in huge wooden casks in the belly of the ship.)

- Whaleboats were about thirty feet long and had six-man crews. Once a whale was spotted, the boat was lowered to the surface of the water, and the men took chase. These were the boats used on the famous "Nantucket sleigh rides," an expression given to describe the pursuit of a whale.

Ghosts That Can't Say Goodbye

Unless you are a year-round resident of Nantucket, you may feel a bit gloomy as Labor Day approaches. Summer's end means packing your bags and saying goodbye to the beautiful beaches and your favorite surfboard. No more trips to the ice cream shop or barbeques until next year. Worst of all is saying goodbye to your summertime friends. That is reason enough for anyone to want to stay on Nantucket forever.

This may be the very reason Nantucket is one of the most haunted islands in the country. The ghosts of former residents must have loved Nantucket so much, they didn't want to leave. So, when they died, they did just that: stayed on the island forever.

You can find these "resident ghosts" in the oldest and most historic part of town around Main Street. The ghostly phantoms ramble endlessly across the cobblestone streets, tag along with folks on an evening stroll, or suddenly appear when least expected.

One of these ghostly residents is Mrs. Lydia Barrett, who once lived in a mansion at 72 Main Street. Her home was one of the most beautiful in all of Nantucket. In 1846, a devastating fire destroyed much of the town. With the wind-blown flames racing through the streets, the fire marshal decided to blow up some of the houses to slow down the out-of-control blaze.

With Mrs. Barrett's house in the direct path of the blaze, the firefighters ordered her to leave. She stood in the doorway with her hands on her hips. She declared she was not leaving: they would have to blast the house with her inside.

At the last minute, the wind changed direction, and her house was saved. It still stands today and is one of the most beautiful historic homes on Main Street.

According to many witnesses, Lydia Barrett *also* continues to stand guard at the mansion. People frequently report seeing an apparition of a woman in a billowing 1850s gown greeting visitors to the house. Even today, she is often seen drifting throughout the house, inspecting her beloved possessions.

Another specter seen moving across the cobblestones is that of famous Nantucket astronomer, Maria Mitchell. As a child, she lived in the top-floor apartment over the bank where her father was a teller. After being given a telescope, she spent countless hours exploring the heavens. Her interest in astronomy grew, and in 1847, she became the first American—and first woman—to discover a comet within our solar system.

Now, on clear nights, just as the sun sets, visitors may see the specter of the famous astronomer scurrying up the ladder to the roof of the bank building where she kept her telescope for so many years.

Sarah Bunker was self-reliant, like many women of old-time Nantucket. Local women held down many jobs when their husbands were away at sea for months at a time. They not only had to raise the children and run the household, but they also oversaw the family's finances, kept the house in good condition, and dealt with emergencies.

Sarah worked caring for the sick and dying. She delivered babies and used herbs to cure illnesses and heal wounds. She carried a small lantern to light her way as she made her nightly rounds to those in need.

When she was eighty, she had a serious fall and could no longer care for others. Although she spent the rest of her life in her upstairs bedroom, she never lost her strong personality and became quite fussy and demanding of her caretakers.

She was ninety-three when she died in 1902. Although she had spent thirteen years couped up in that upstairs bedroom, she decided to stay on after she passed. According to eyewitnesses, each day, her pearly white shadow floats down the main staircase to take part in afternoon tea. After hovering near the tea table for a few minutes, the presence drifts silently up the staircase and disappears into her old bedroom.

You never know who you might meet on a dark, foggy night on Nantucket. There is a chance you could meet a famous athlete, actor, or rock star. But beware . . . that famous person may not be a living person at all.

You could meet the specter of a well-known former sea captain from Nantucket's whaling days. He will not look like a captain of a mighty ship, for these days, his withered and bent frame shuffles across the cobblestones wearing an old-fashioned watchman's uniform. Only those who peer closely at his face see that he hardly has a face at all.

But this is no ordinary specter. It is the ghost of George Pollard, who some claim is the unluckiest sea captain in all of Nantucket. He was the captain of the whaling ship the *Essex*, which sank in 1820 after it was rammed by a giant sperm whale. The captain and crew were set adrift in the middle of the Pacific Ocean, thousands of miles from shore. Many months later, another whaler rescued the starved and scraggy men and returned them to Nantucket.

Not long afterward, Captain Pollard took command of *Two Brothers*, the very ship that had rescued him in the Pacific. But his good luck was not to last. Soon after he became captain, the ship ran aground and sank. Once

again, the captain was rescued and returned to Nantucket.

After surviving this second sinking, George Pollard never again returned to sea. He took a job as a night watchman, walking the Nantucket harbor for the rest of his life.

Although he has been dead for more than 150 years, the grayish specter of the sea captain still haunts the island. If you look closely, you might spot him standing on the steps of the Jared Coffin House on Broad Street as if waiting for someone. More often, he trudges along the cobblestone streets of downtown, still dressed in his faded blue captain's uniform.

These hauntings are only a few of the peculiar and spooky specters you may encounter on Nantucket. Like so many, they love the island and simply can't say goodbye.

NANTUCKET TIDBITS:

- Nantucket was devastated in 1846 by a huge windblown fire. Hundreds of people lost both their homes and jobs. Many left the island and never returned.

- Many of the older homes on the island are haunted. Some owners are unwilling

to share stories of their haunted houses. Others are delighted to share the antics of their ghosts with you. Some will even make up stories to be part of the spooky fun.

- Always be very polite when asking about someone's haunting. Many people regard their resident ghosts as family.

CHAPTER 6

The Windblown Ghosts of the Old Mill

The Old Mill has been perched atop the highest point on Nantucket Island for as long as anyone can remember. That doesn't come as a surprise because it was built nearly three centuries ago! Today, it's one of the best-known landmarks in all of Nantucket.

Local folklore says the Old Mill was built by Nathan Wilbur in 1749. Soon after, it was sold to the Swain family, who ran the mill for more than eighty years. Those who ran the gristmill (a mill for grinding grain) were known as millers. They needed to be highly skilled. The gears, cogs, levers, and pulleys in the mill were not only complicated but also downright dangerous. One slip up and a miller could lose an arm, a leg, or even his life.

The windmill was successful for many years, but the relentless Atlantic winds and

harsh New England winters took their toll on the tower. By 1829, the Old Mill was little more than a pile of kindling. Although Jared Gardner bought the Old Mill for firewood, he changed his mind, restored it, and ran it for a while as a working gristmill. Other owners operated the mill afterward, and soon it became a tourist attraction.

The Nantucket Historical Association purchased the Old Mill in 1897. Today, visitors can tour the historic mill and even watch demonstrations as corn is ground into cornmeal, just as it was in Nantucket's early days. If they are lucky, visitors will also catch a peek of one of the numerous ghosts known to prowl the old tower.

No one denies that the Old Mill is haunted. But you may be surprised by the number of ghosts spotted at the site. The ghost of Nathan

Wilbur, who designed and built the mill, has been seen roaming the old tower. His out-of-focus form pays no attention to the living; it just scurries around making invisible repairs.

Local folklore says he built the tower with wood retrieved from one of the many shipwrecks found along the Nantucket shore. That may explain why ghostly ragged figures dressed in old seamen's garb often trail Wilbur's ghost around the mill.

The mill has had many owners over the last 275 years, and it seems many of them are still around. They want to make sure the mill is being run properly, and they want us to know they are still around. Modern-day volunteers at the mill must stay alert. They never know when a ghost might decide to adjust the mill's settings. Ghosts have been known to both slow down *and* speed up the milling, causing the entire building to rattle and shake.

One of the spirits you're likely to meet here is the ghost of Timothy Swain. Like his father, he successfully ran the mill for several years. That is, until one morning, when his lifeless body was found inside. Timothy was dead, but the mill was running at full speed. No one knows why he'd run the mill alone in the night's darkness, yet there was no sign of foul play. All anyone knows is that Timothy died in the mill ... and it seems he has never left! Although he likes to move things around, Timothy's ghost does not choose to interact with the living.

Not everyone who visits the old mill will encounter a ghost—just the lucky ones.

NANTUCKET TIDBITS:

- The gray-colored Old Mill on Nantucket is called a smock mill because it has eight sides that are narrow at the top and wider at the bottom, like old smocks or aprons used to be. It stands fifty feet high and has four thirty-four-foot wooden vanes attached at the top. As these rotate clockwise in the wind, they move the old stone that grinds the hard corn kernels into flour.

- People don't usually think about ghosts when they first look at the old windmill. It reminds them of how hard it was to survive during the earliest days on the island. In 1746, the Mill immediately became one of the most important places on Nantucket. Making flour from corn is backbreaking and time-consuming work. Everyone must have been overjoyed when the Mill finally made that job easier and faster. It could grind five bushels (280 pounds) of corn into flour in just one hour. That job would take many days by hand.

- The Old Mill is a popular tourist site and an important historical site on Nantucket. You can watch as 300-year-old tools grind corn into flour.

CHAPTER 7

Happy Hauntings at The Chicken Box!

If you love honey-fried chicken with all the fixings, The Chicken Box on Dave Street is the place for you. Located about a mile and a half from the historic district, it is like no other restaurant on Nantucket. People come from around the world to munch on the famous Southern fried chicken and listen to live music. Although it was once a small one-room shack, it has become one of the busiest restaurants on the island.

The first owners were Willie and Lena House, a young African American couple who came to the island to work for a wealthy family in 1949. Shortly after, Willie opened the little eatery serving Southern-style fried chicken in a shack that had been used for many purposes through the years. It quickly became a gathering spot for others who worked on the island. His first customers were housekeepers, chauffeurs, gardeners, harbor workers, and farmers. As word spread about Willie's delicious food, The Chicken Box became nearly as famous as Nantucket itself.

But the building where The Chicken Box is located already had some notoriety. In 1920, Congress passed an unpopular law called the Prohibition Act, which made it illegal to make, sell, or transport alcohol anywhere in the United States. It was such an unpopular law that most people simply ignored it.

All across the East Coast, smuggling alcohol—often called rum running—became big business. Nantucket was no different. Nearly everyone on the island who owned a boat made extra money by hauling barrels of outlawed brew to shore.

Secret meeting places known as speakeasies popped up all over the island. People drank the smuggled alcohol and danced to the latest music. It wasn't long before the shack where The Chicken Box now operates became one of the most popular speakeasies in town.

Many of the reports of hauntings here are from the Prohibition Era. After all, this law against alcohol went on for thirteen long years. Ever since, there has been gossip about unexplained sightings and ghostly apparitions at the popular restaurant.

One well-known account of a haunting stems from the days when the building housing The Chicken Box was a busy speakeasy. One visitor reported seeing a group of three ghostly apparitions dressed in 1920s attire loitering near the loading dock. As he watched, they began to shove a large wooden barrel toward the restaurant's rear door. The oversized container was so heavy, it took all three just to roll it along the dock.

Finally, the group was able to shove it onto the back porch. While two of the men kept watch, the other tapped softly on the door. It opened just enough for a pair of eyes to peek out into the night.

The men nodded at one another without speaking. The door swung open and the men quickly shoved the huge barrel through the doorway. Instantly, the door banged shut. The three ghostly figures disappeared into the night without a trace.

Ever since, this apparition has been reported by visitors and staff at The Chicken Box. Ghosts from this unhappy time have continued haunting this out-of-the-way address for over a hundred years.

The ghosts here like to play tricks on the restaurant workers. They make a mess of the cutlery drawers and push things off tables.

They sometimes cause arguments among the staff. The chef knows exactly how many chicken wings are on a platter when he hands it to the waitress. But often by the time the platter reaches the guests, it is half empty. The chicken wings have disappeared.

Guests become angry because their plates are half full. Waitresses are blamed for stealing the wings. When this happens, the staff always finds the missing chicken neatly stacked in a pile on a shelf by the back door.

Most spirits at The Chicken Box seem to enjoy the different kinds of music echoing throughout the restaurant. Apparitions of pale figures dancing to the music are common. Performers have even been the target of mischievous ghosts. Sometimes electric guitars suddenly lose power, microphones go dead, or amplifiers screech uncontrollably although they are unplugged.

Today, The Chicken Box is a busy restaurant and a popular music venue. People line up around the block during the summer to catch their favorite bands and enjoy the honey-dipped chicken.

The thousands of people who flock here each summer are not the least concerned about ghosts. They are so busy enjoying the food and music that they barely notice any mischievous spirits who might be there.

You will be in for a treat if you are lucky enough to go to The Chicken Box for lunch. You just might see a ghost, if you can take your eyes off the scrumptious chicken on your plate.

NANTUCKET TIDBITS:

- The Chicken Box has been serving its delicious honey-fried chicken for nearly seventy-five years. That's tens of thousands of drumsticks, wings, and chicken fingers!

- Some of the most famous jazz, blues, reggae, and rock musicians perform at the "The Box" each season. Tickets for musical events usually sell out far in advance.

CHAPTER 8

Ghosts from Beneath the Sea

The Nantucket summer season was in full swing on the sunny Thursday of July 25, 1956. The hotels were busy, the beaches were full, and no one was prepared for what was about to happen.

Just after sunset, a murky blanket of clouds settled across the island. It was the kind of fog that islanders know well. The white haze was so thick and heavy that it felt like a weight on your shoulders. The streets quickly emptied as everyone headed indoors. Along the shoreline, boats of all shapes and sizes bobbed gently in their moorings. Only a foolish sailor would risk being out on the water on a night like this.

International shipping lanes begin at sea a few miles from the island. They mark the safe passage for vessels from around the world traveling to New York Harbor. As the fog set in, ships in these lanes went on alert. Speeds decreased, fog horns blared, and crews rushed to their lookout positions.

Among the traffic using the shipping lanes that night were two ocean liners. Westbound from Europe was the 700-foot-long passenger liner, the *Andrea Doria*. With 1,200 passengers and a crew of 575, the luxury liner was moving steadily toward New York. The Swedish liner *Stockholm* was not far away but traveling in the opposite direction. She was sailing eastward in the opposite direction from the *Andrea Doria* with 747 passengers and crew onboard.

It was an accident that everyone said should never have happened. Although both vessels had modern navigation equipment, neither ship could see farther than their bow. The ships were sailing blind. Both liners tried quickly changing course to avoid the collision, but it was too late.

The *Stockholm* rammed the side of the larger ship, instantly killing fifty-one people (five on the *Stockholm* and forty-six on the *Andrea Doria*). Within minutes, the *Andrea Doria* rolled on her side and began to fill with water. Both ships sent out SOS signals giving their exact location with an urgent request for ships to rescue passengers. The moment ships in the vicinity heard the distress call, they raced to help.

Although half of the *Andrea Doria*'s lifeboats

were already under water, the captain had no choice but to give the order to "man the remaining lifeboats." Since the *Stockholm* was not in danger of sinking, she immediately took on passengers from the *Andrea Doria*. In less than an hour, more than fifteen ships had arrived, and within hours, they rescued more than 1,600 people.

As the fog cleared the next morning, the *Andrea Doria* slowly sank below the surface of the water. The *Stockholm* limped back to shore for repairs, and the passengers and crew were on their way back to New York.

People did not know then that ghostly

spirits from the wreck would haunt Nantucket for many years to come!

The carcass of the *Andrea Doria* has been resting on the ocean floor not far from the Nantucket Lightship for more than sixty years. The wreck draws divers from all around the world. Some want to do scientific research, others want to recover valuable objects from the site, and some divers just want the honor of saying they have explored the famous shipwreck.

The wreck does not give up its treasures easily. It lies in the middle of the busy international shipping lane. Treacherous currents and shifting sands from the bottom make it nearly impossible to see under the water.

Some even say that the wreck site is cursed. Since 1956, more than twenty highly trained ocean divers have lost their lives at this wreck site. Some perfectly healthy divers suddenly suffered heart attacks or died for unknown reasons during their searches of the *Andrea Doria*. Although experts inspect the expensive diving gear before every single dive, equipment failure is often the cause of diving accidents. Divers do sometimes get snagged on wreckage or whacked by floating debris, but it is strange for physically fit divers to just pass out underwater.

In addition to these dangers, divers have reported some very strange experiences while exploring the wreckage. A few have reported seeing phantom passengers, dressed in fancy clothes, rush toward them as if seeking help. Other ghostly figures ignore the divers, moving about the wreckage as if it were still afloat.

Ghostly arms have been seen reaching out of portholes,

grasping at anyone or anything that swims by. Others say they hear crying and whimpering from these same windows. Doors that have been rusted shut for decades pop open without warning, and sometimes there is the faint sound of garbled voices.

One group reported hearing the distinct sounds of music echoing around the wreck, but they couldn't identify what kind of music they were hearing. But in another case, the witnesses heard an accordion playing a popular dance tune. This is especially bone-chilling because in the cargo hold of the *Andrea Doria* was a shipment of accordions bound for a music store in New York City. Although the wreck has been explored in detail, not a single accordion has been found. Perhaps the spirits of the sunken ship have formed their own band?

The wreck site of the *Andrea Doria* is one of

the most famous shipwrecks in the world, with many skilled divers eager to explore the site. Although some who have already braved the dangerous wreck would happily do so again, other divers would not repeat their dive for any amount of money.

What do you think? Is the *Andrea Doria* dive site cursed? Are the remains of the grand old liner really an underwater home for ghosts? You decide.

NANTUCKET TIDBITS:

- The *Andria Doria* was once called a floating art museum because it carried dozens of valuable artworks on the day she sank.

- After a complete makeover, the *Stockholm* returned to service with a new name, the *AV Astoria*. She is the oldest passenger liner still in service today.

- The SOS from the stricken vessels brought no fewer than fifteen ships, as well as aircraft to offer assistance. Saving people from a sinking ship in the open ocean is difficult. With more than 1,600 lives saved, the rescue mission is one of the most successful in history.

CHAPTER 9

Haunted Hotels and Spooky Inns

Nantucket was not always as beautiful as it is today. Although it may be hard to believe, the island has suffered hard times. When the whaling industry died, the jobs disappeared, forcing many people to move off the island. In 1846, Nantucket suffered one of its greatest tragedies. Just as summer was in full swing, a devastating wildfire spread across town.

It destroyed a third of the town, burned hundreds of buildings, and left many homeless.

Nantucket quickly rebuilt. Within a few years, people started coming to the island during the summer to escape the dirt and grime of the cities. Boarding houses and hotels popped up around town and across the island. Twenty-five years later, popular magazines such as Sribner's began promoting it as a destination.

Today, there is no trace of the fire or of hard times on the island. The streets are lined with beautiful homes, hotels, and charming shops. Visitors return year after year to enjoy the slow-paced life, spotless beaches, and charming hotels.

People often ask why Nantucket has so many haunted places, especially haunted hotels. It's true that many hotels and inns are home to rambling spirits, strange apparitions, and unexplained happenings. Ghosts are known to wander corridors, float across public rooms, interrupt performances, and even invade guest rooms! Although a few hotels disbelieve the claims of hauntings, nearly all are aware of their resident spooks and are happy to talk about them.

One of these was first called Breeze Point Hotel. It has welcomed guests to Nantucket for more than a hundred years. Today, the sprawling gray-and-green-shingled hotel is known as The Nantucket Hotel and Resort. In its early days, the hotel was famous for its big band nightclub and afternoon concerts on the lawn. This may be why witnesses have seen the ghostly apparitions of old-time band members lurking around the hotel. Sometimes, a faint melody echoes throughout the hotel, drifting from the hallways into the guest rooms. As the music begins, a ghostly woman in a shimmering red dress often appears near the old dining room, as if waiting for the band to play.

Guests report a spooky presence following them as they move around the hotel. One man said he was about to sit on a wicker chair on the porch when he suddenly felt the strange sensation that it was already occupied. He immediately jumped up and moved to a nearby bench because something just was not right.

You don't have to go far to find more haunted hotels in the center of Nantucket. In fact, there is a cluster of haunted inns on a single block facing India Street. The small guesthouses look more like a little village than a single hotel. Yet, each inn has its own name as well as its own ghosts.

The Roberts House is the most famous. It was built in 1846 after the great fire. Its crisp white paint, black shutters, and cozy, sheltered porch make it easy to spot. Although stories about the ghosts of the Roberts House have been known for years, not all the modern-day staff will admit to the hauntings. The ghosts here are so well known that the Nantucket Ghost Tour stops here during every outing.

One of the best-known ghosts lives in the Roberts House basement. She is a young woman with long hair, and she's dressed in a nightgown. Some ghost hunters claim she seems afraid. Others say misty apparitions dart along the upper hallways, while many guests claim someone watches them as they sleep. One desk clerk admits that people often ask for a haunted room when making a reservation.

Nearby, in the Meeting House, guests staying in room 209 often call down to the desk in the middle of the night. They complain that loud arguing from a nearby room is keeping them awake. When the staff investigates, they find there's no argument going on. In fact, the rooms on either side of 209 are empty!

Still, many guests have reported the problem over recent years. They all agree they here a person saying, "But, but, Mrs. Williams!" It remained a mystery until recently when a former owner revealed that the land on which the Meeting House now stands was once the site of a cottage owned by a lady named Mrs.

Williams. It seems her ghost has remained behind to continue the argument.

Another inn close by is Manor House. This beautiful hotel is well known for its ghostly visitors. Most reports come from the third floor, where guests report feeling that they are not alone. To make matters worse, doors and windows open and close by themselves.

A carpenter repairing a wooden banister was certain he saw a ghost. He finished fixing the banister and carefully locked the doors and windows as he left the building. When he turned to look back at the inn, he saw a woman staring back at him from an upstairs window. He raced back into the building, but the pale-faced figure was gone.

The newest building on the street is the Gate House Hotel, built in 2013. Although only about ten years old, the Gate House was crafted to look like all the other New England-style buildings in the area.

It may come as a surprise that it already has its share of ghostly visitors. The first reports came from the workmen building the new hotel. The electricians complained when their power tools would not work. Batteries suddenly lost power, tools were lost or misplaced, and the paint refused to dry.

Many of Nantucket's inns and hotels have their own resident ghosts, and many will happily share their latest antics. For the most part, these ghostly visitors are mild-tempered, agreeable, and even friendly. Perhaps they just want us to know they are here, or maybe they love the island so much that they refuse to leave.

No matter where you are on Nantucket, keep a sharp eye out for one of the many ghosts that dwell on the island. But remember, if you happen to stay in one of the island's famously haunted hotels . . . you just might have a ghost as a roommate!

NANTUCKET TIDBITS:

- The worst fire in Nantucket's history broke out in July 1846. It started in the stovepipe of a hat shop but quickly engulfed Nantucket's wharves, factories, and businesses. Driven by powerful winds, the fire burned for more than seven hours, gobbling up every market and shop in town. Seven factories and twelve warehouses were destroyed. Three of Nantucket's four wharves were destroyed, and 800 islanders lost their homes.

- Did you know that only 14,000 people live on Nantucket year-round? Life is always a bit slow-paced on the island, but it is *especially* quiet during the winter, when most of the restaurants, shops, and entertainment venues close down. After all, New England winters are harsh and bitterly cold. Yet, when summer arrives, more than 80,000 people call Nantucket home. (Talk about night and day!) If you are here in the summer, you're sure to find countless things to do, like swimming, boating, and visiting the island's many shops, hotels, music venues, and restaurants. But if you're here in the winter, well . . . be sure to bring a couple of good books!

A Ghostly Goodbye

What do you think about Nantucket's ghosts, specters, and unexplained happenings? Do you agree that Nantucket is one of the most haunted islands in the North Atlantic?

If not, how would you explain the mysterious sightings such as Pastor Seth chasing the noisy boys from the church? Or the ghostly figures seen smuggling rum through the back door of The Chicken Box? Not to mention, the spirits from the *Andrea Doria* shipwreck roaming the island at will, and the ghost of the island's unluckiest sea captain keeping watch along Nantucket harbor.

Perhaps you don't believe in ghosts. Maybe you are a person who has to see something to believe it. If so, you might want to walk around the island and stop at some of the haunted places described in this book. Nantucket will not disappoint you, for it is as haunted as it is beautiful.

Expect countless adventures and to make new friends on your jaunt around the island. You will meet many interesting people; some will be living, and others will be dead. But there is nothing to worry about. Everyone knows that ghosts love to make new friends.

Patricia Heyer is a coastal history buff with a special interest in folklore and marine science. She has written extensively for both children and adults during her career. Her most recent title, *Jaws of the Jersey Shore* was released in 2024. Pat is an avid reader, beachcomber, and animal rescue supporter. She resides on the Jersey shore with her husband, Rob, and their rescue cat, Gracie.

Check out some of the other *Spooky America* titles available now!

Spooky America was adapted from the creeptastic *Haunted America* series for adults. *Haunted America* explores historical haunts in cities and regions across America. Here's more from the original *Haunted Nantucket* author, Barbara Sillery: